I, Doll

by Nara Ai, Nara Walker

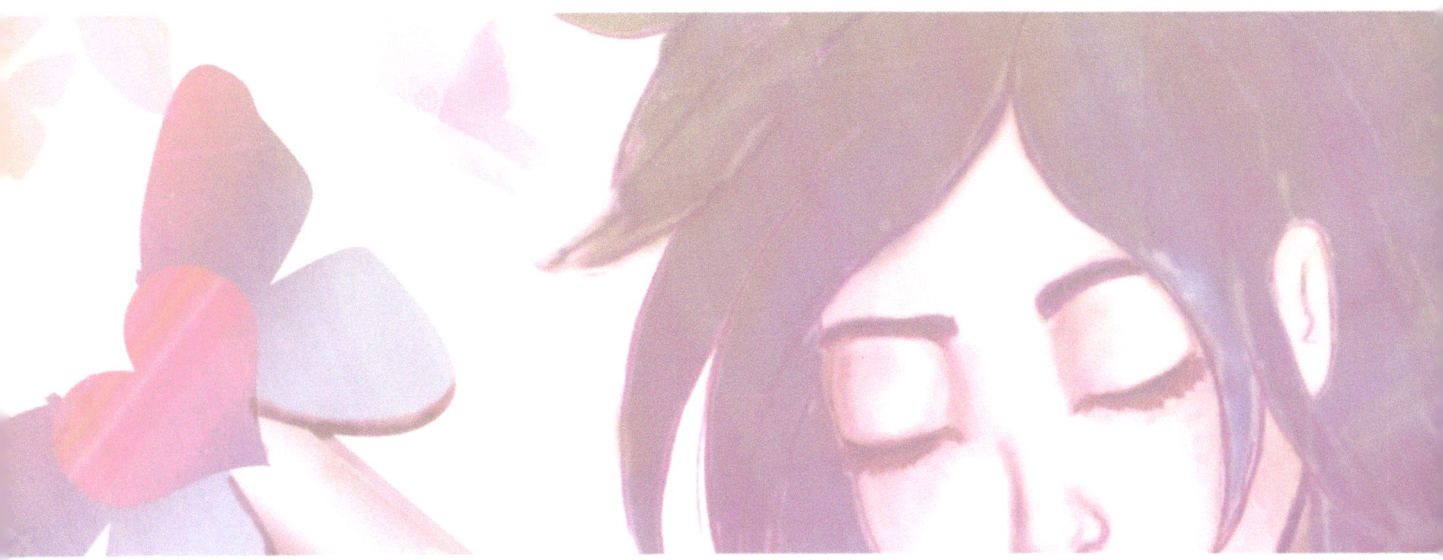

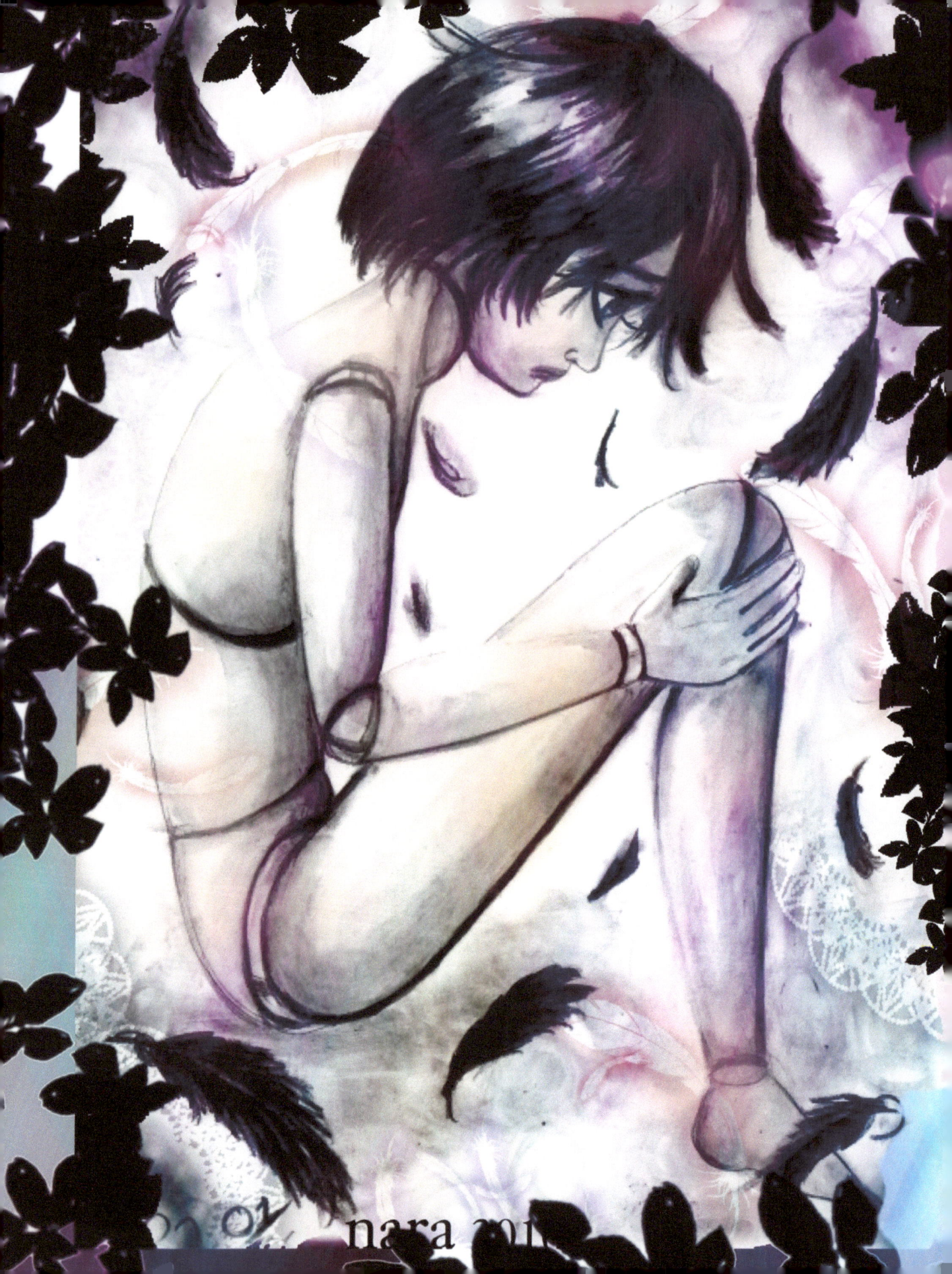

nara mi

Can I count you like the sands?
I feel slipping through my hands.
I want to hold you like a ray...
Of some long forgotten day.

I want this moment to always   last
I'd give up the future to relive the past.

Can I hum you like a tune?
I forgot just all to soon.

I'd carve your name with in my heart
        If it meant we'd never part...

Can I sing you to the stars?
Sometimes
you seem that
far

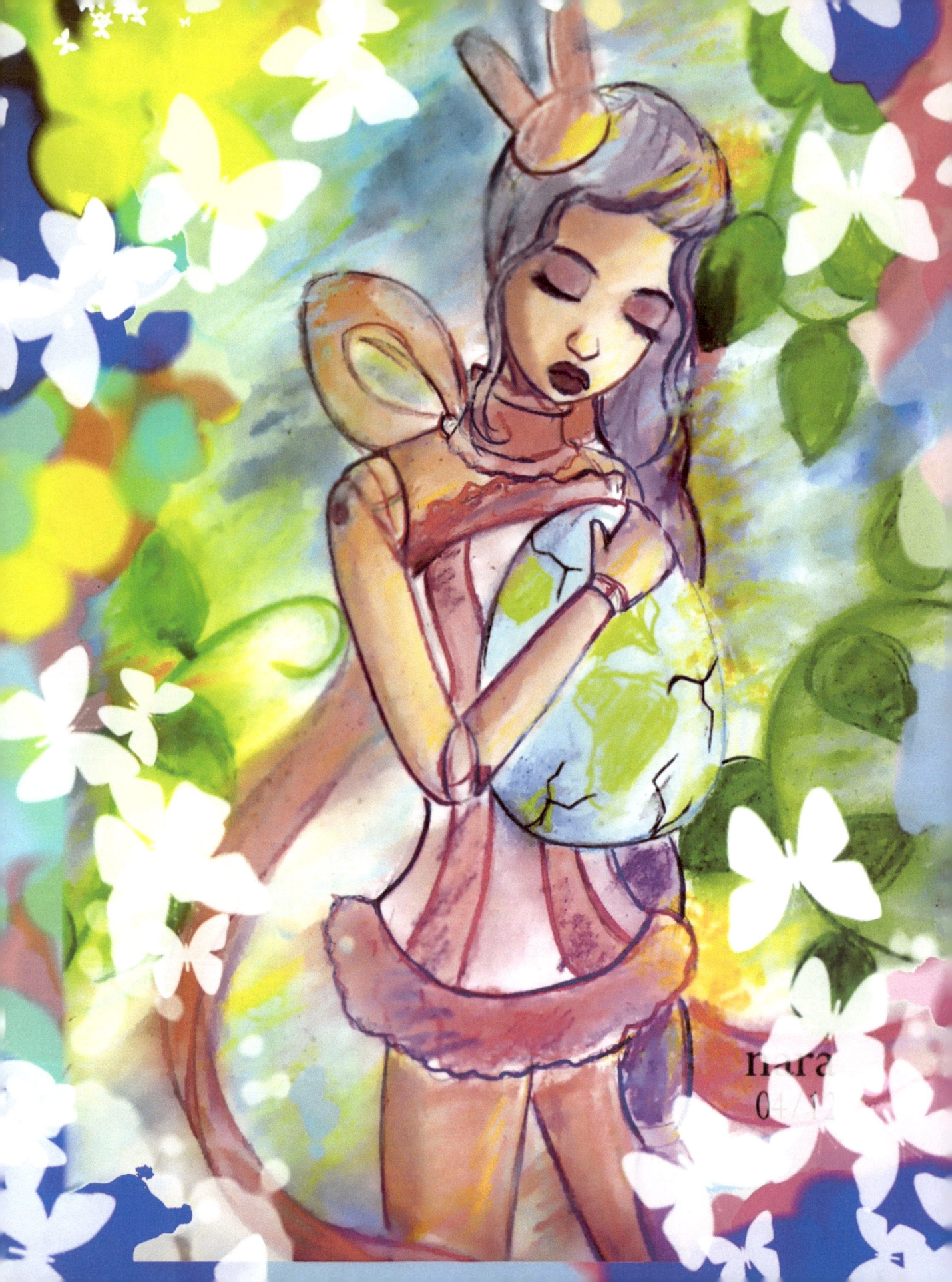

Do you recall?
When you lost it all?
And those tears began to fall. They never did stop.
Now you're drowning in the drops.

I know it's not real.
But it's still how I feel

It blocked out everything.
Overshadowed the sun.
It became the only thing.
You became the only one.

It killed the sky above.
And massacred all I love.
Doesn't matter if it's not real.
Because it's all I feel.

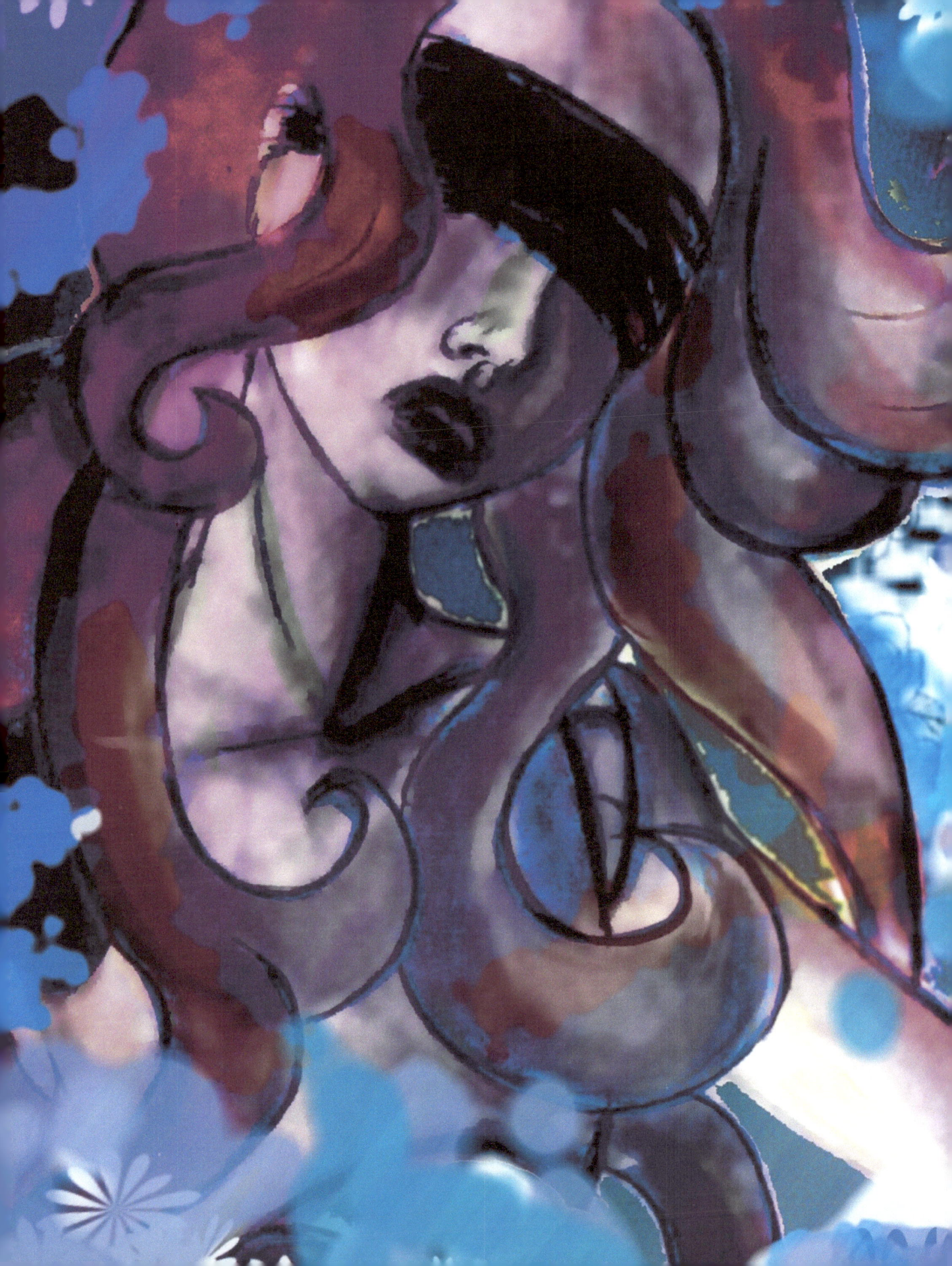

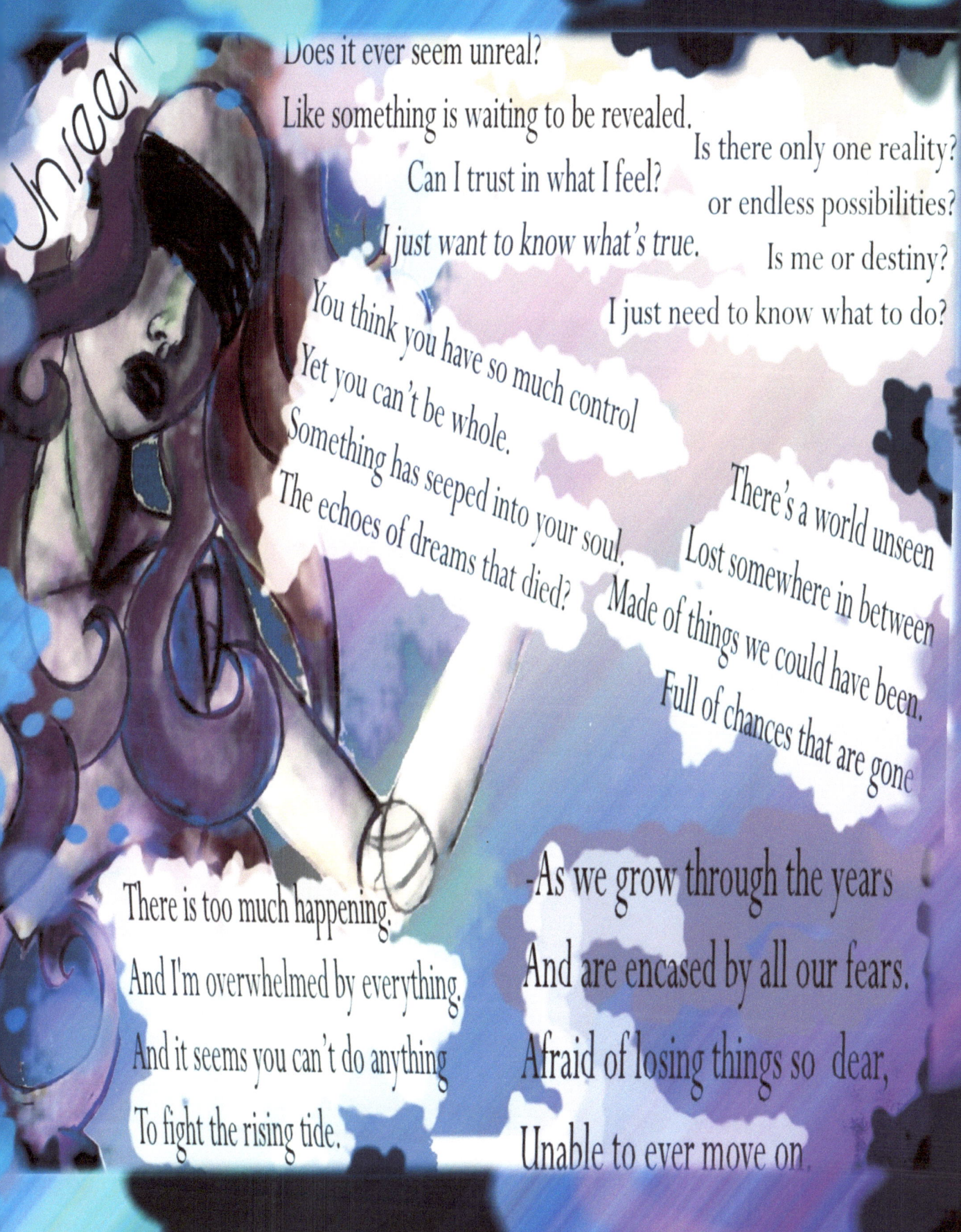

Unseen

Does it ever seem unreal?
Like something is waiting to be revealed.
Is there only one reality?
or endless possibilities?
Can I trust in what I feel?
I just want to know what's true.
Is me or destiny?
I just need to know what to do?

You think you have so much control
Yet you can't be whole.
Something has seeped into your soul.
The echoes of dreams that died?

There's a world unseen
Lost somewhere in between
Made of things we could have been.
Full of chances that are gone

There is too much happening.
And I'm overwhelmed by everything.
And it seems you can't do anything
To fight the rising tide.

-As we grow through the years
And are encased by all our fears.
Afraid of losing things so dear,
Unable to ever move on.

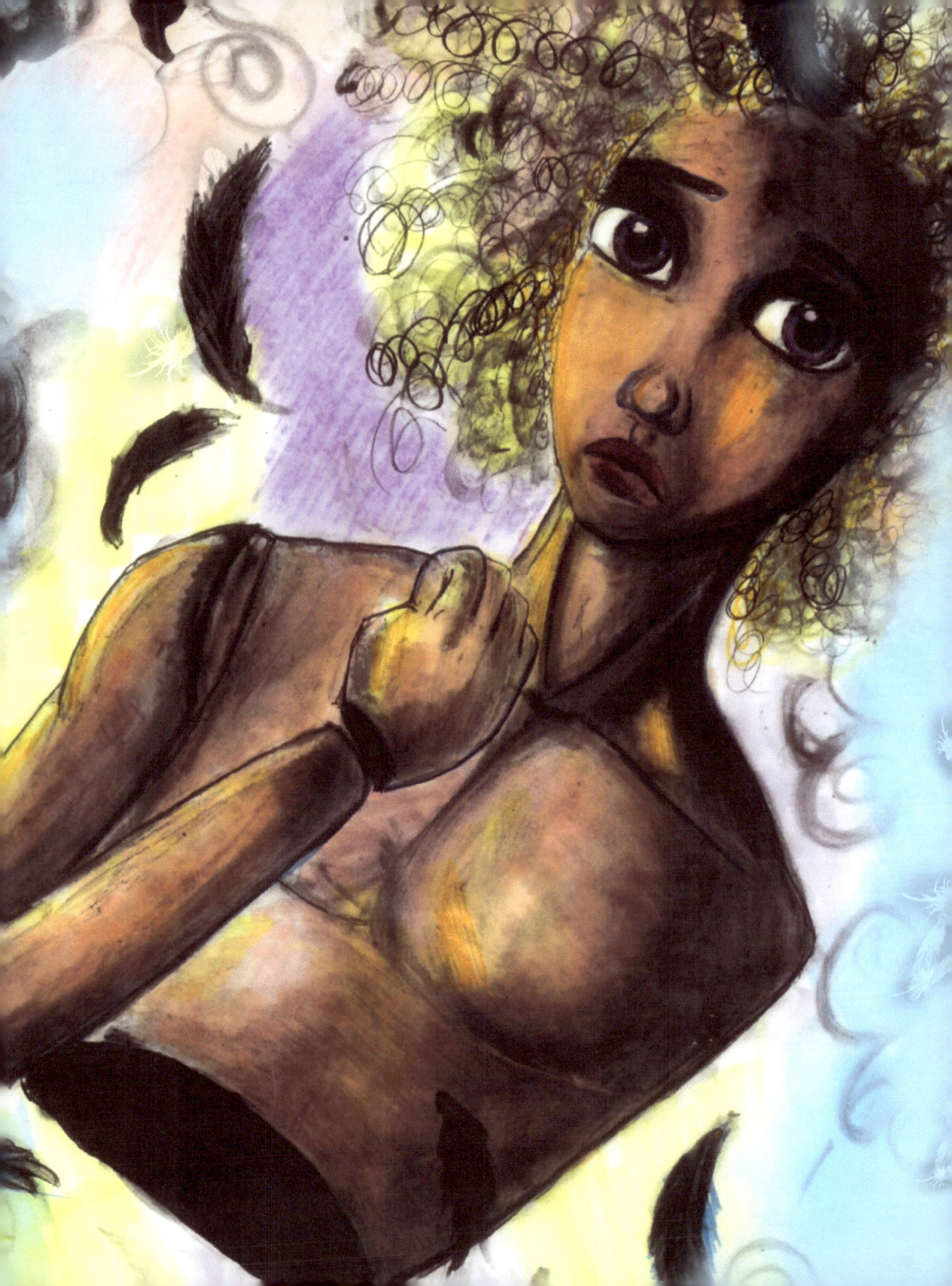

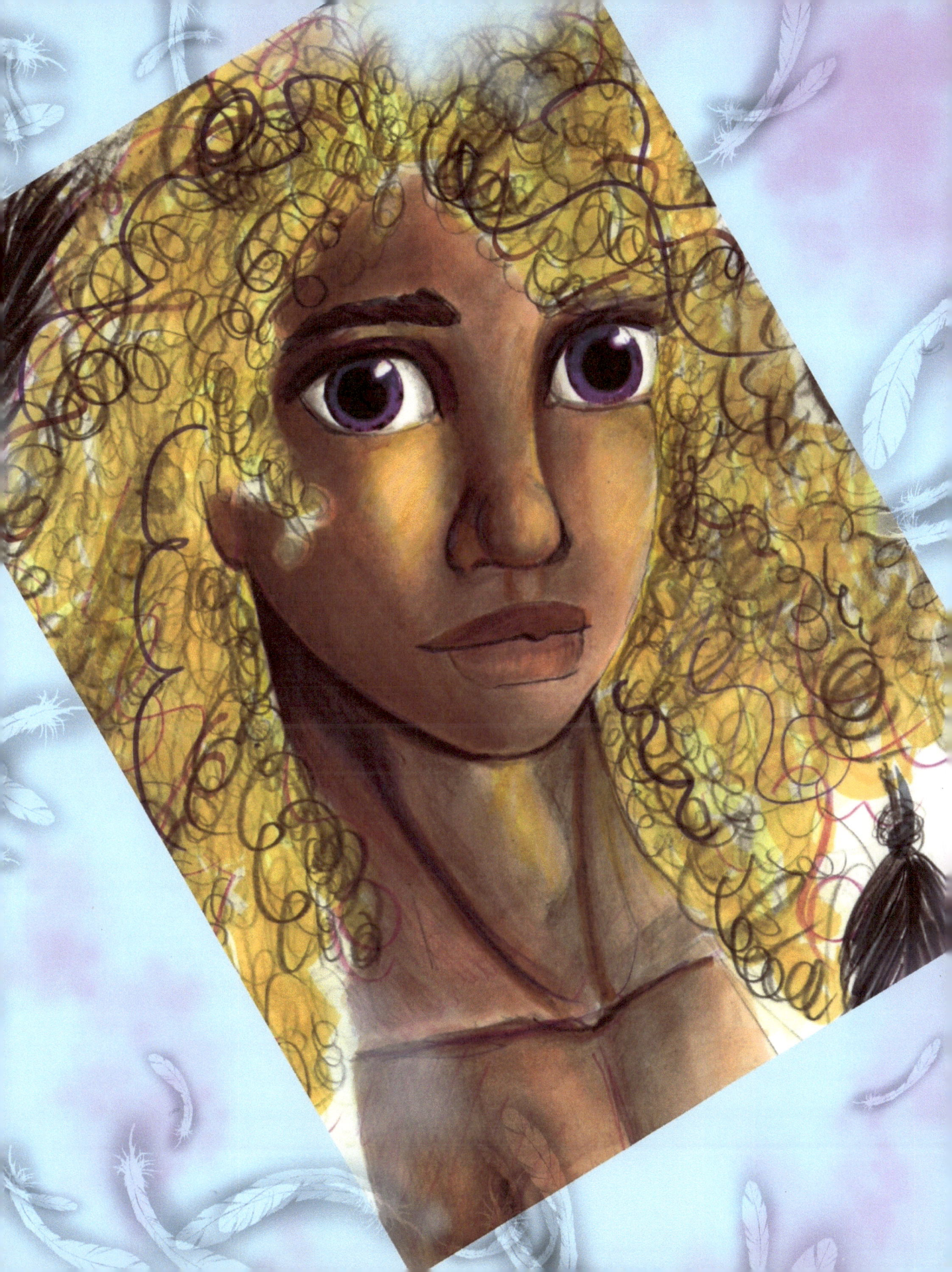

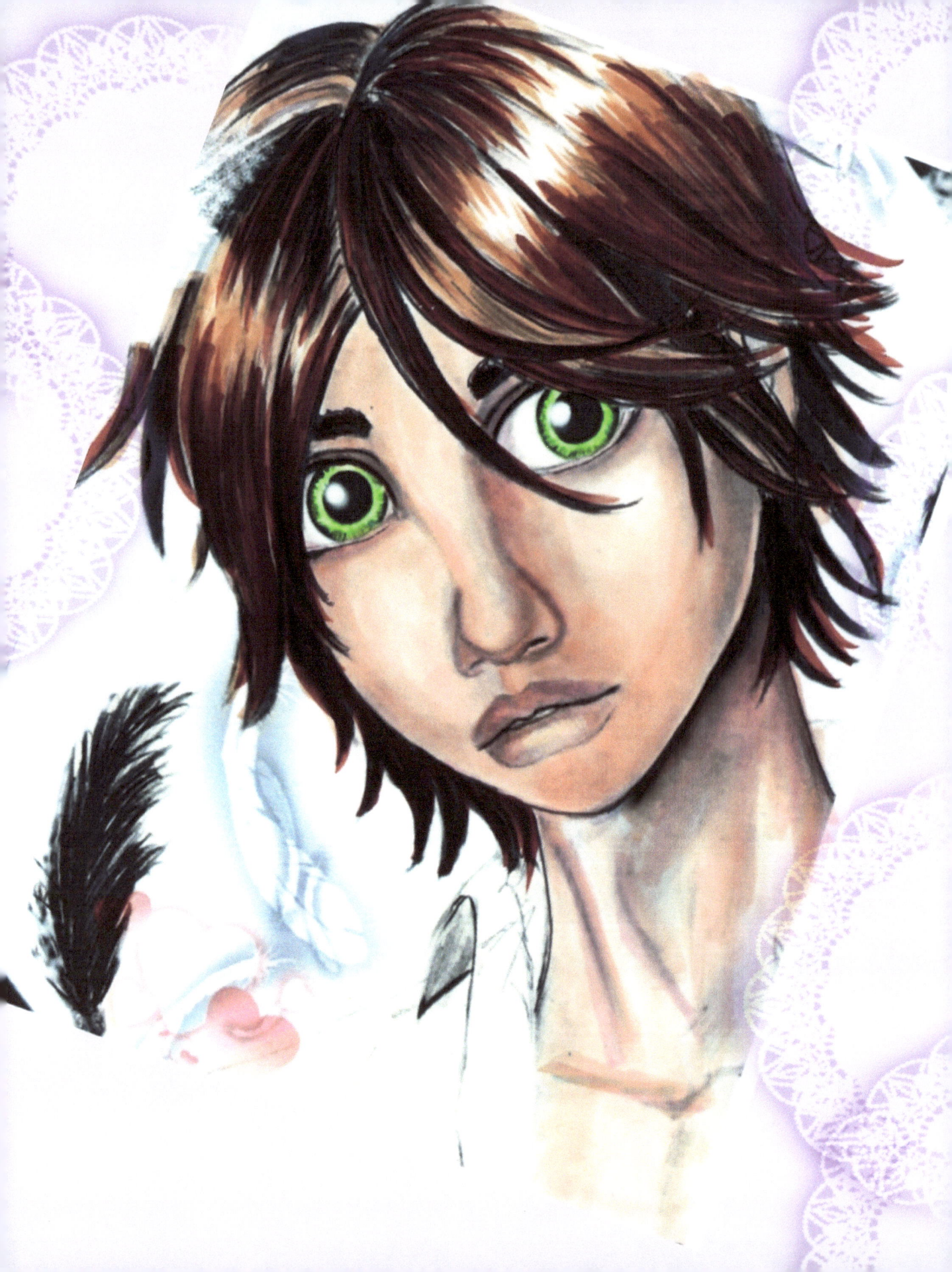

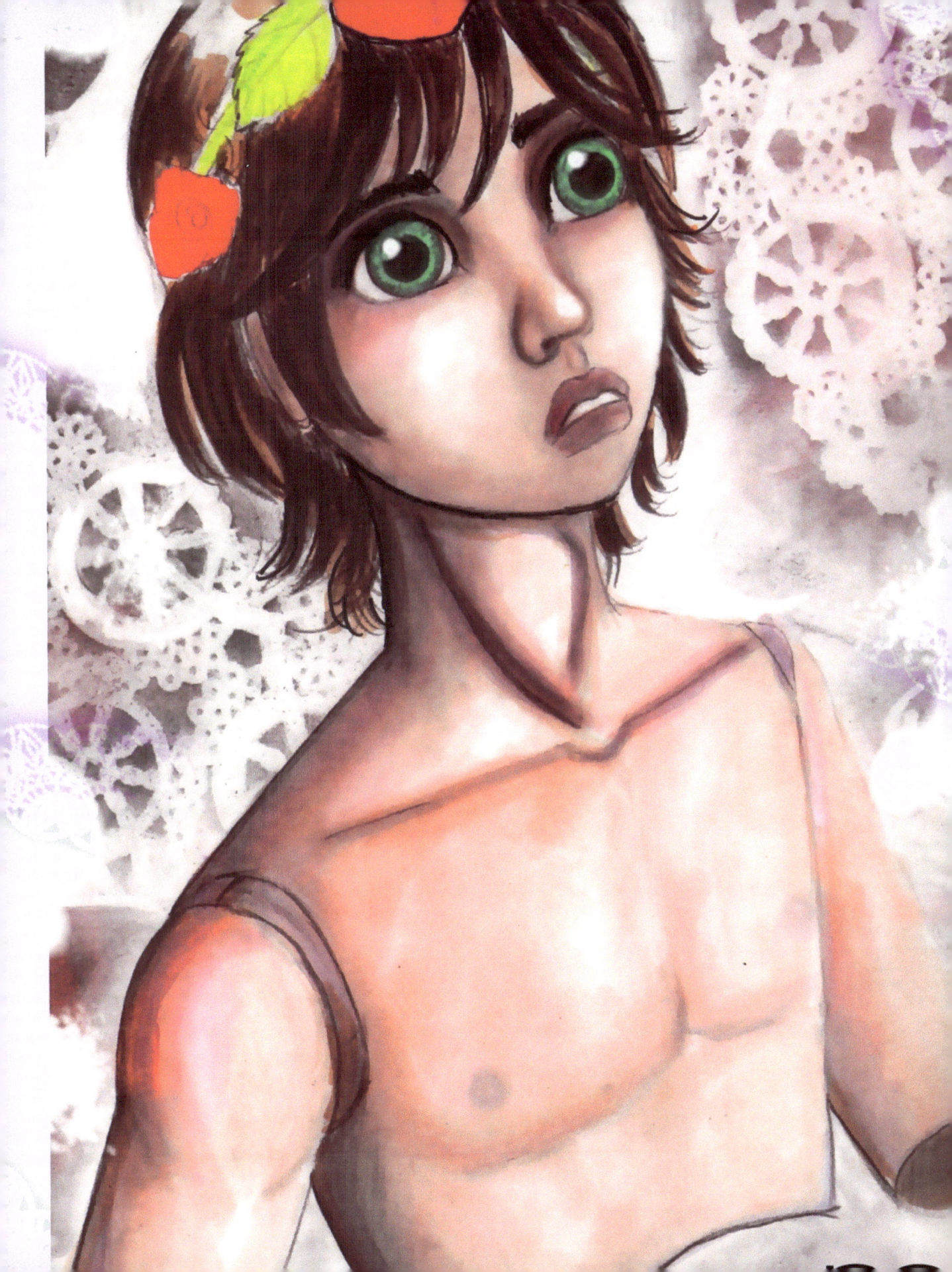

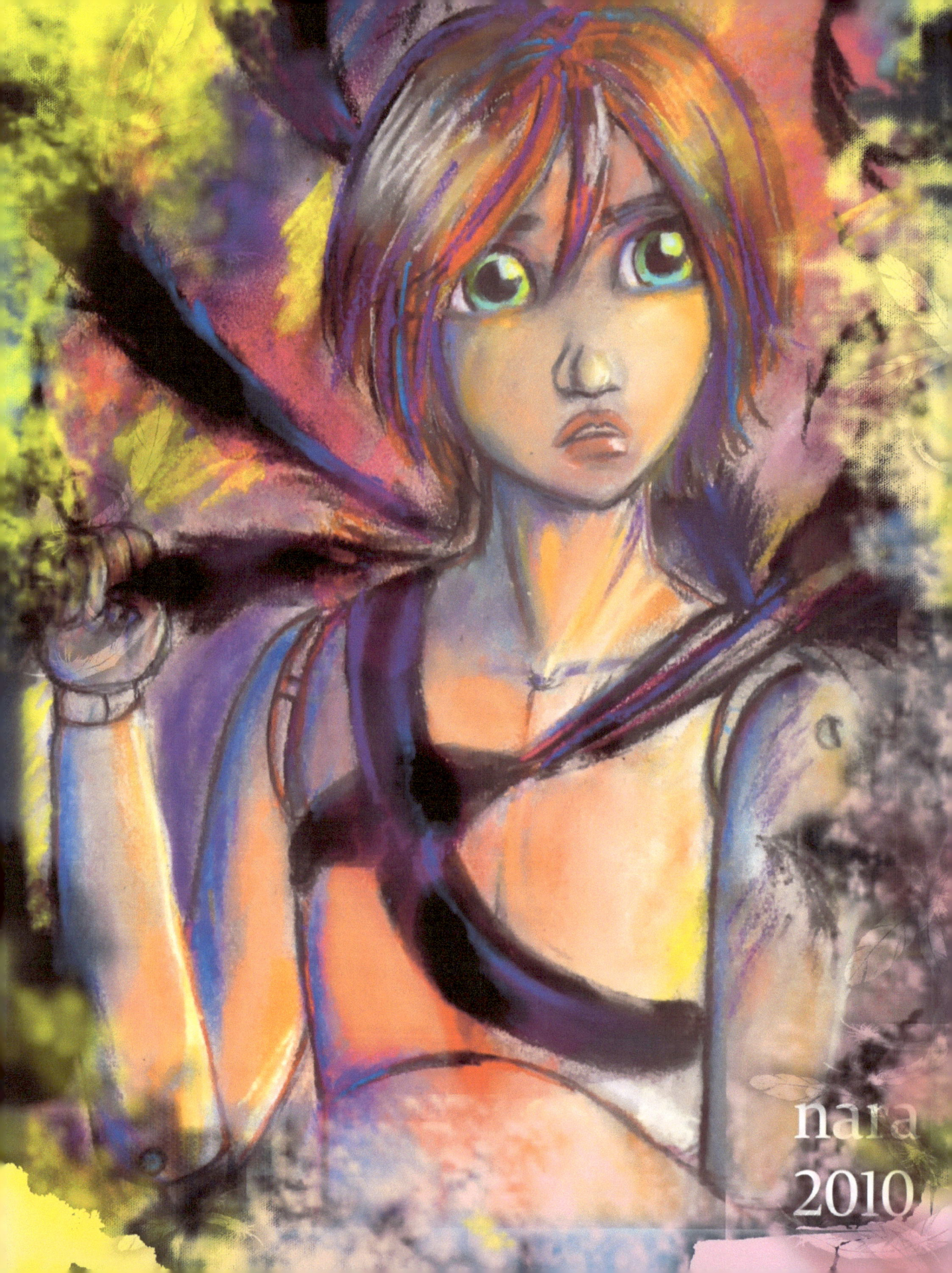

nara
2010

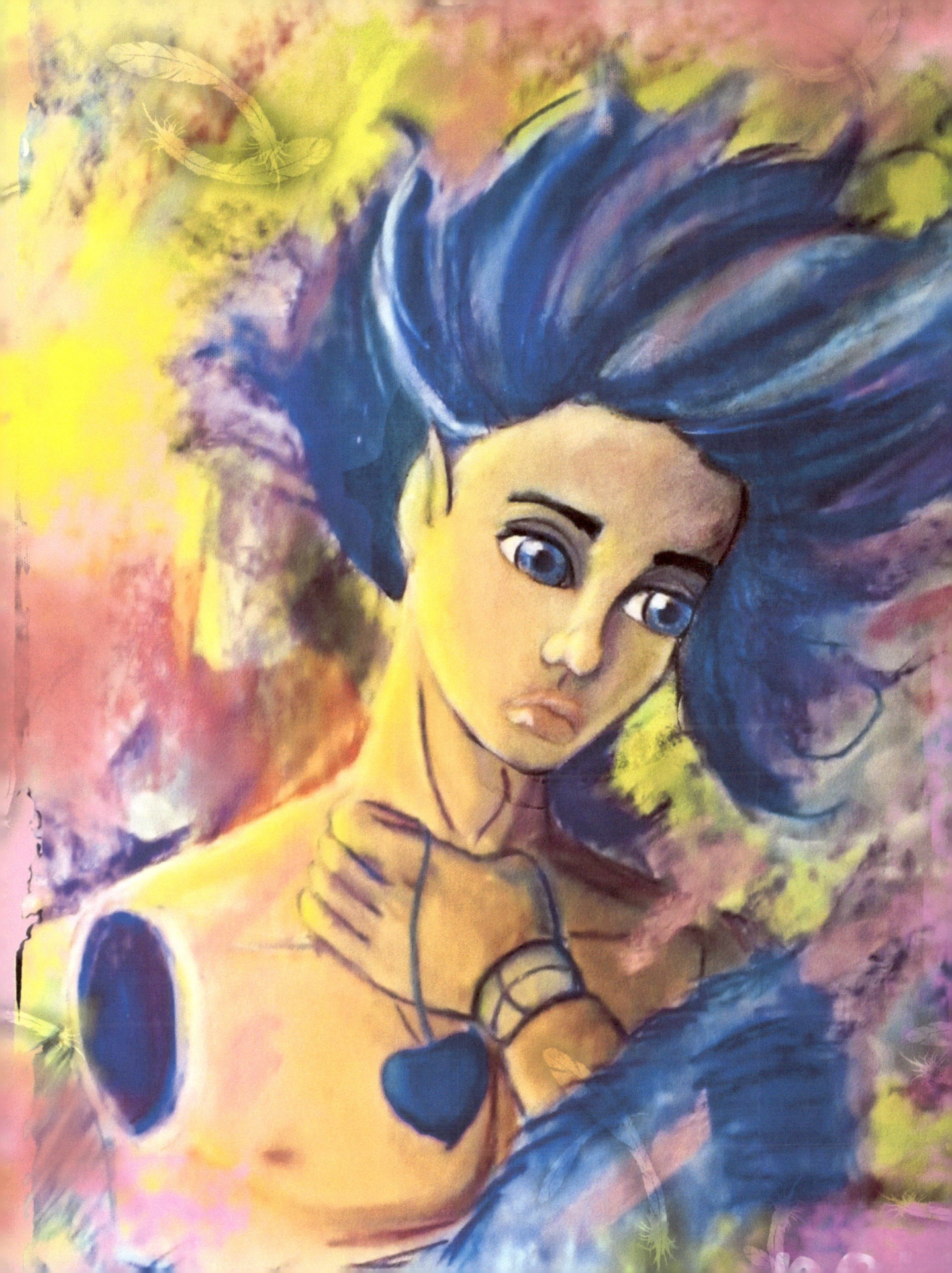

I swear upon angels above
You are all that I'll ever love.
Just one fleeting moment-
-is worth an eternity of torment

I'll take on the slings and arrows
I will never let you go.
Even if this destroys us both
I will never break my oath.

To love you and only you no matter the cost.
To love you, only you, even when all is lost.
When there is nothing more and left.
I'll love you beyond my death.

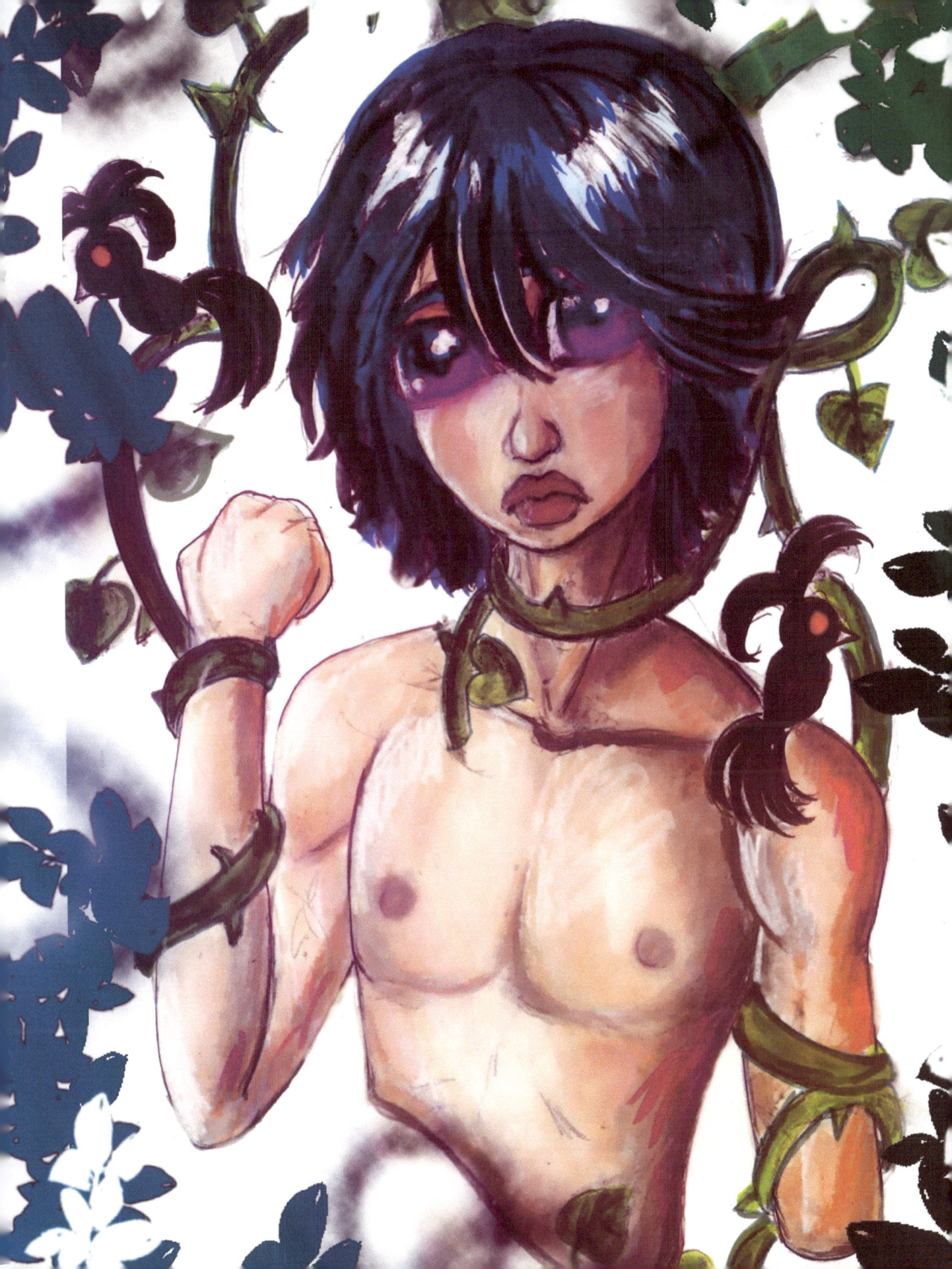

All I want is to be with you.
No matter what is puts me
through...

I will cling to you desperately.
I will defy this destiny
For there will come a time
When I will make you mine

I will never let you go.
Not until you know,
Not until you see.
That you were meant
for me.

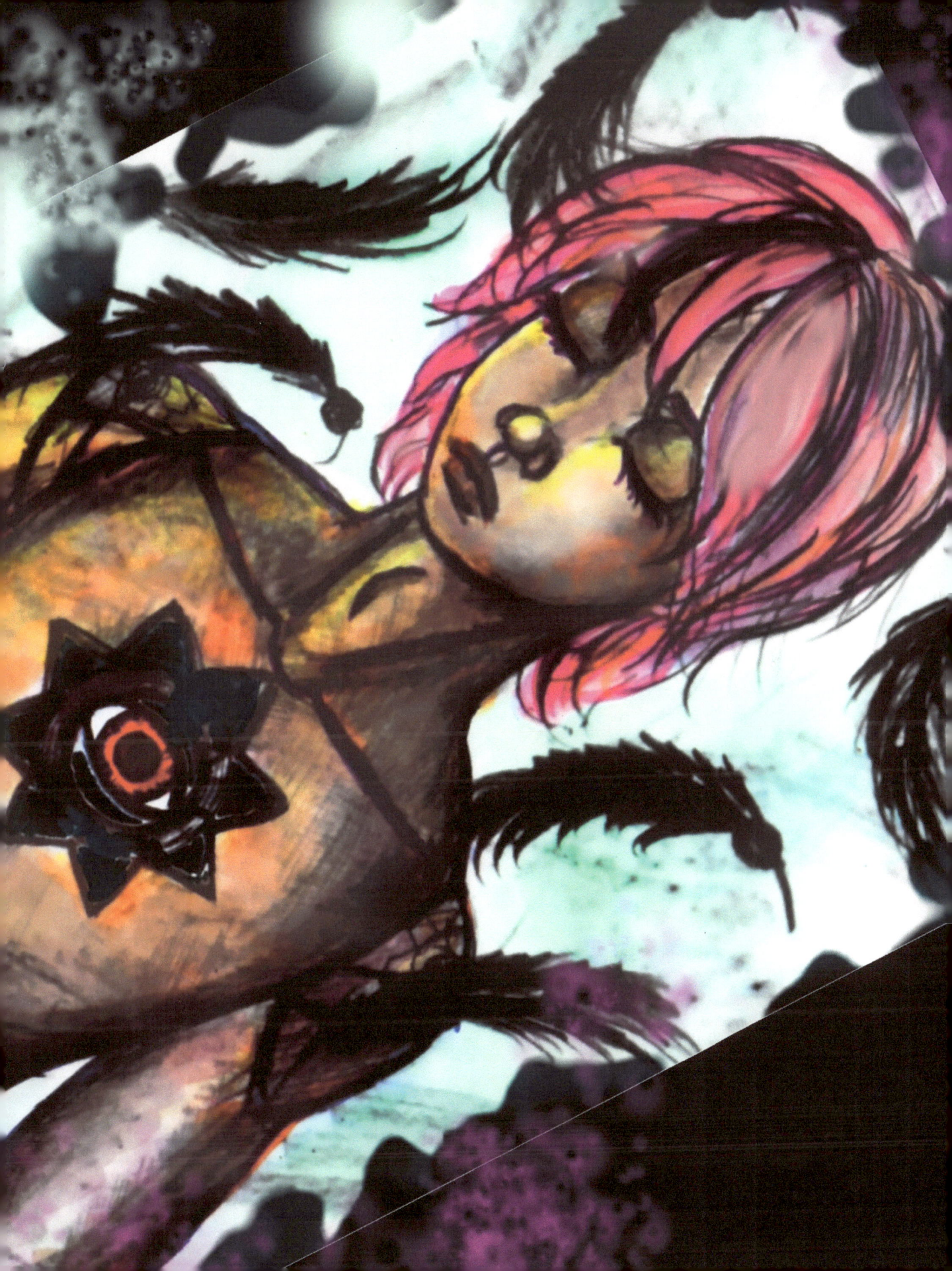

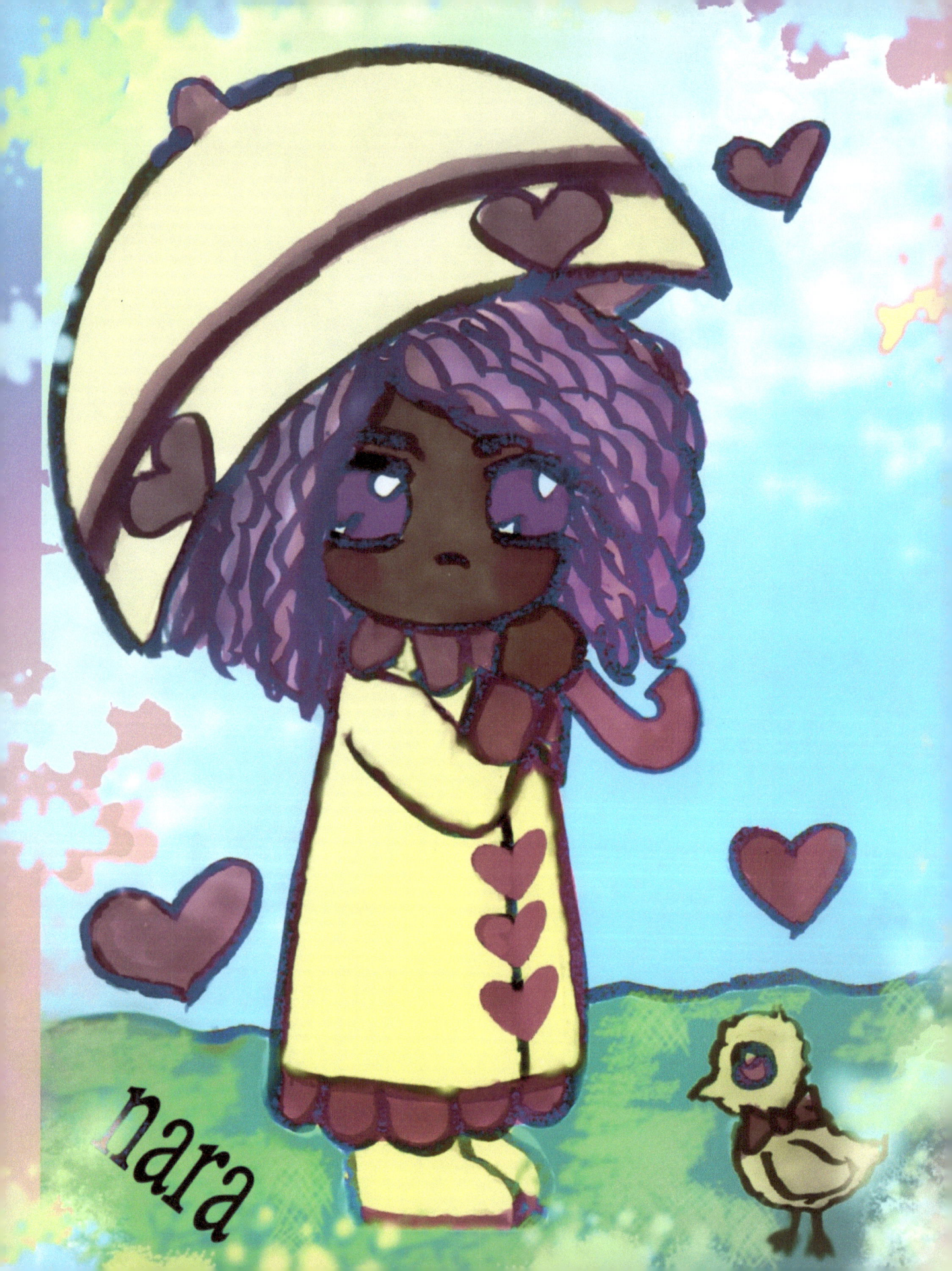

They say children
should be seen and
not heard—

Be Still.
Be Quiet.
Don't say a word.

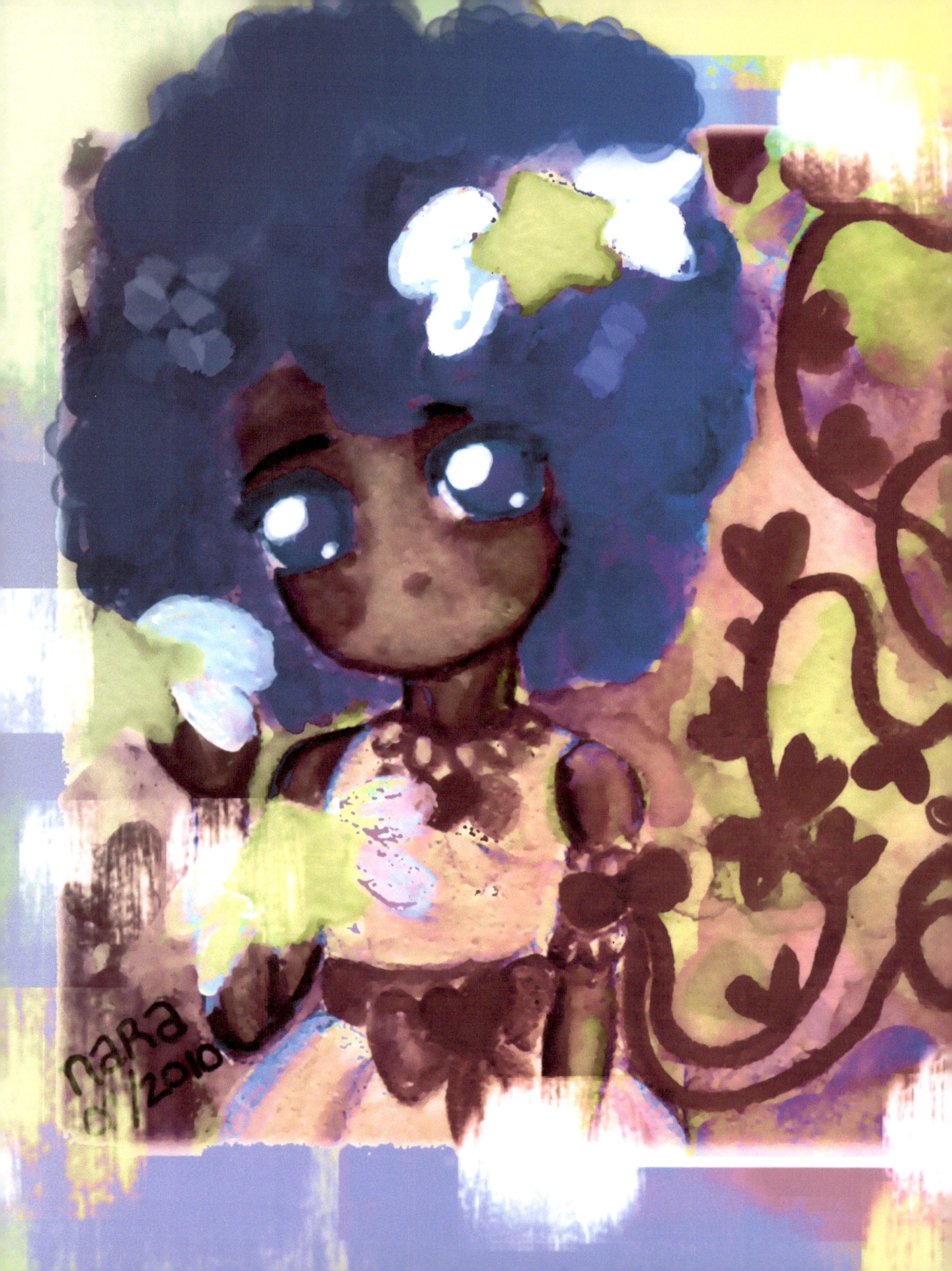

I don't know who you are
but I know that you are a star
Even though I never felt your pain
I know it can't always rain.

When you feel that you're about to break
And there's no more that you can take
It feels like there is nothing left
Not even tears to be wept.

In a world of unending night
In each of us is a light
Together we can bring the dawn
if we just hold on

I know that you're a star

nara 01/10

OUR DREAMS ARE BUTTERFLIES
SOARING HIGH
INTO THE PALE BLUE SKY
SCATTERED BY THE WIND
IT'S ALL COMING TO AN END

WINGS SO BROKEN THEY CAN NEVER MEND.

DREAMS ARE JUST CASTLES IN THE SAND.
AND I CANNOT STAND.
AS THEY CRUMBLE IN MY HANDS.
I CAN DO NO MORE
THE WATER'S OVERFLOWING THE SHORE.
I REALLY THOUGHT WE COULD SOAR.

HERE COMES THE TIDE.
WILL YOU STAY BY MY SIDE?

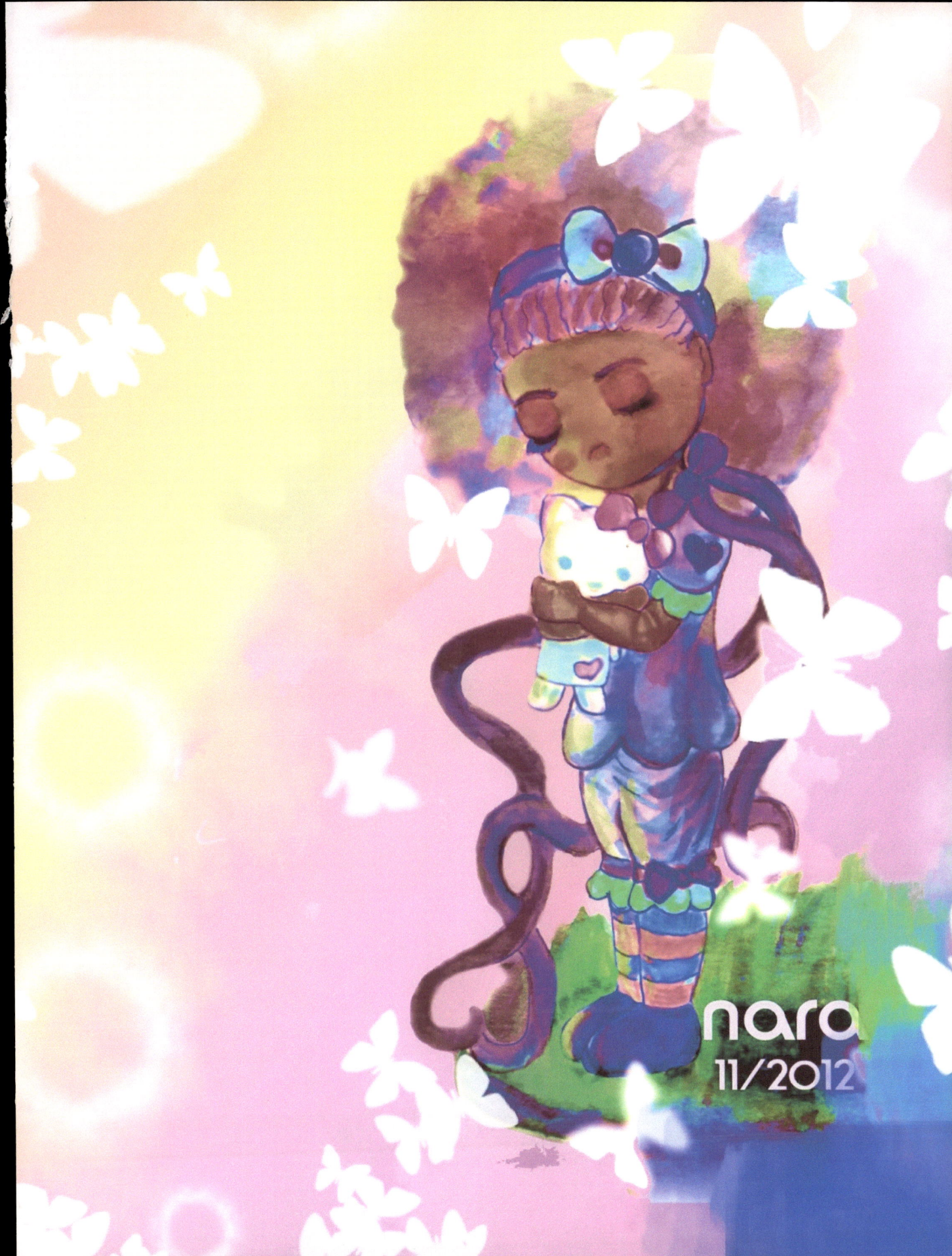

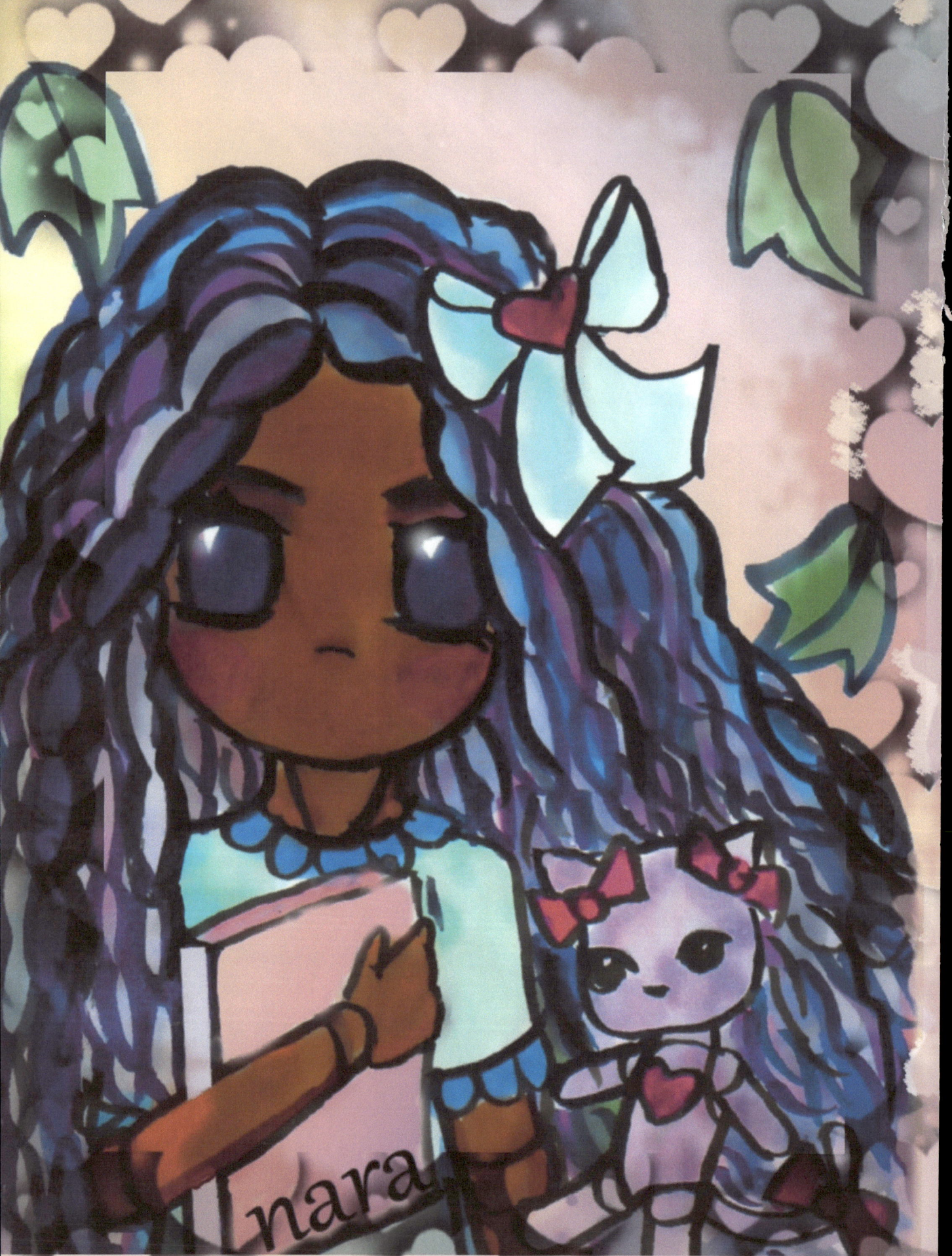

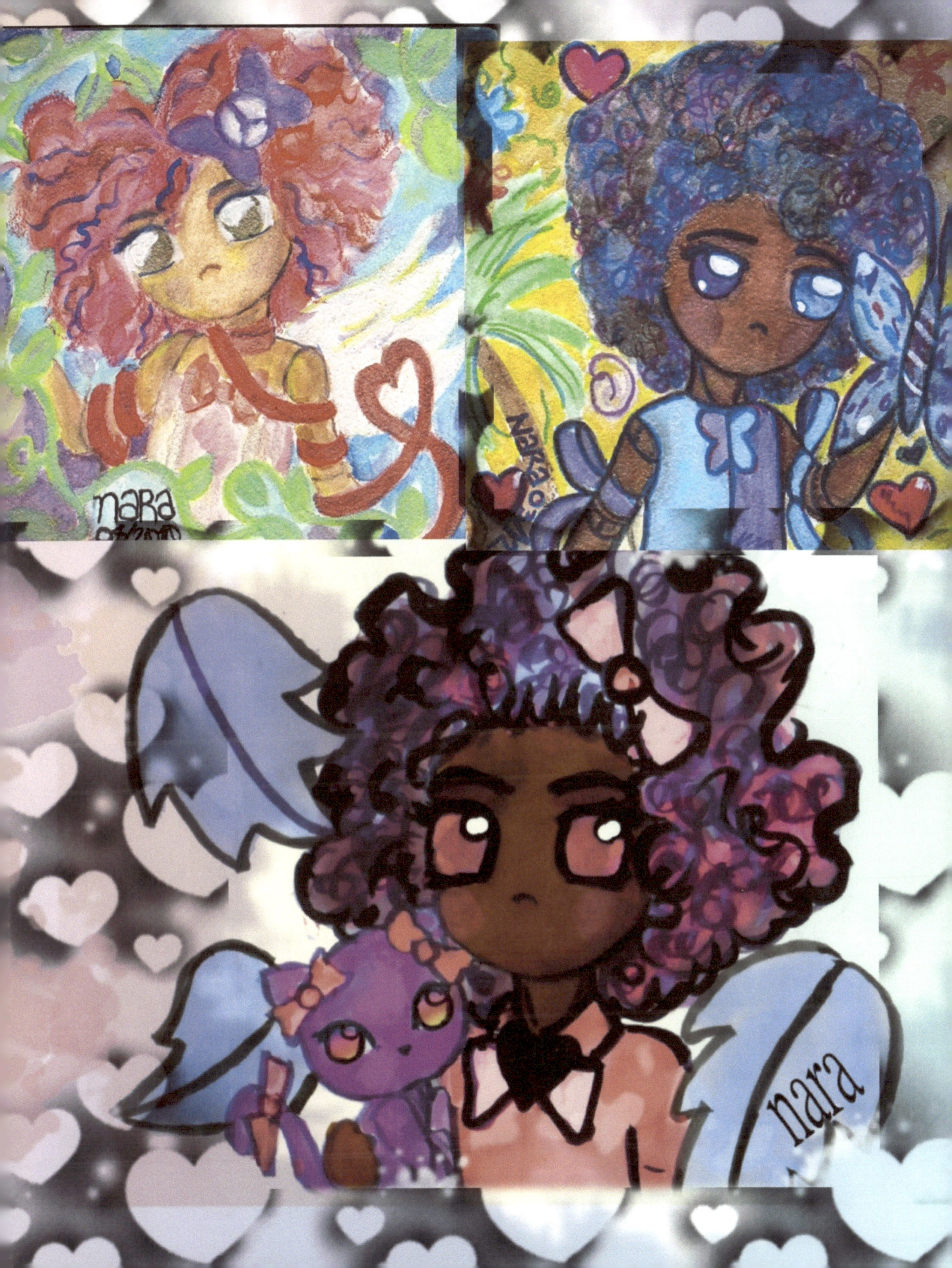

It's not like you say the words that I long to speak.
Or have traveled routes that I now seek.
Or that the stars light up within your eyes.
And then they all fade out when we say goodbye.

My heart doesn't skip a beat

Every time we meet

That's not a wistful sigh

Whenever you pass by

It's not like I carry a picture of you in my heart.

Don't think where you end is where I start.

In love with you? No, I could never fall…

It's not like that, it's not like that at all.

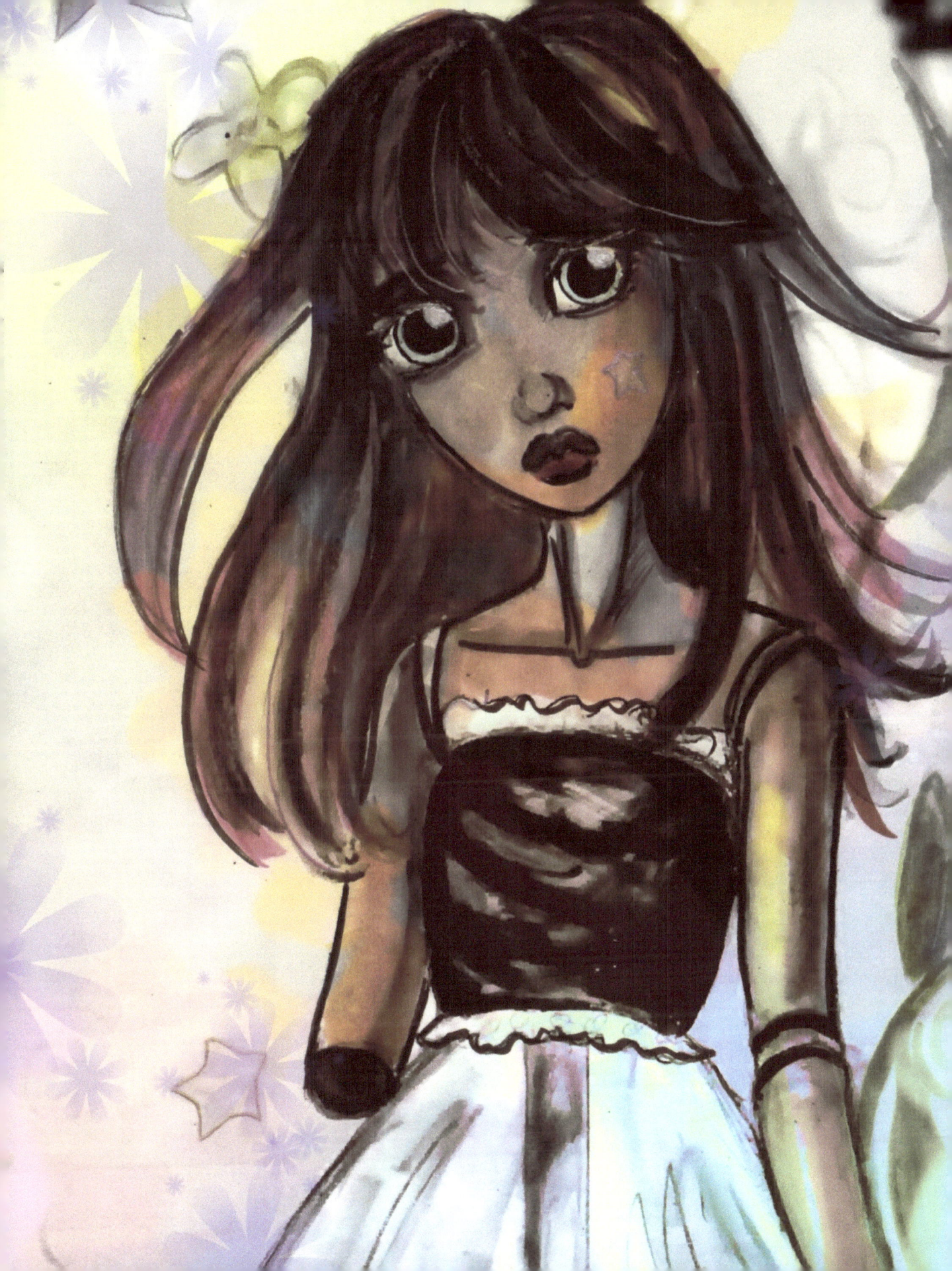

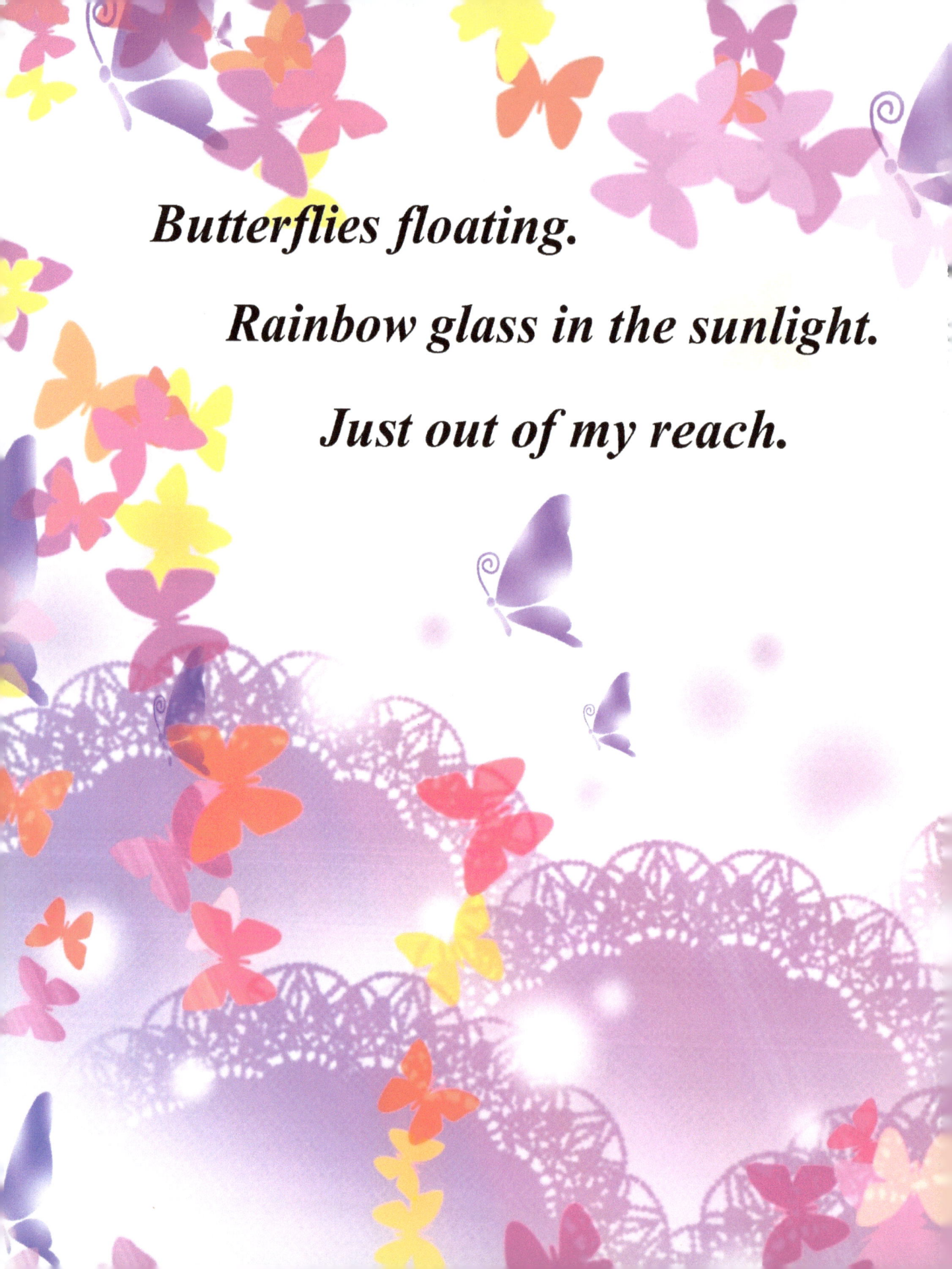

Butterflies floating.

Rainbow glass in the sunlight.

Just out of my reach.

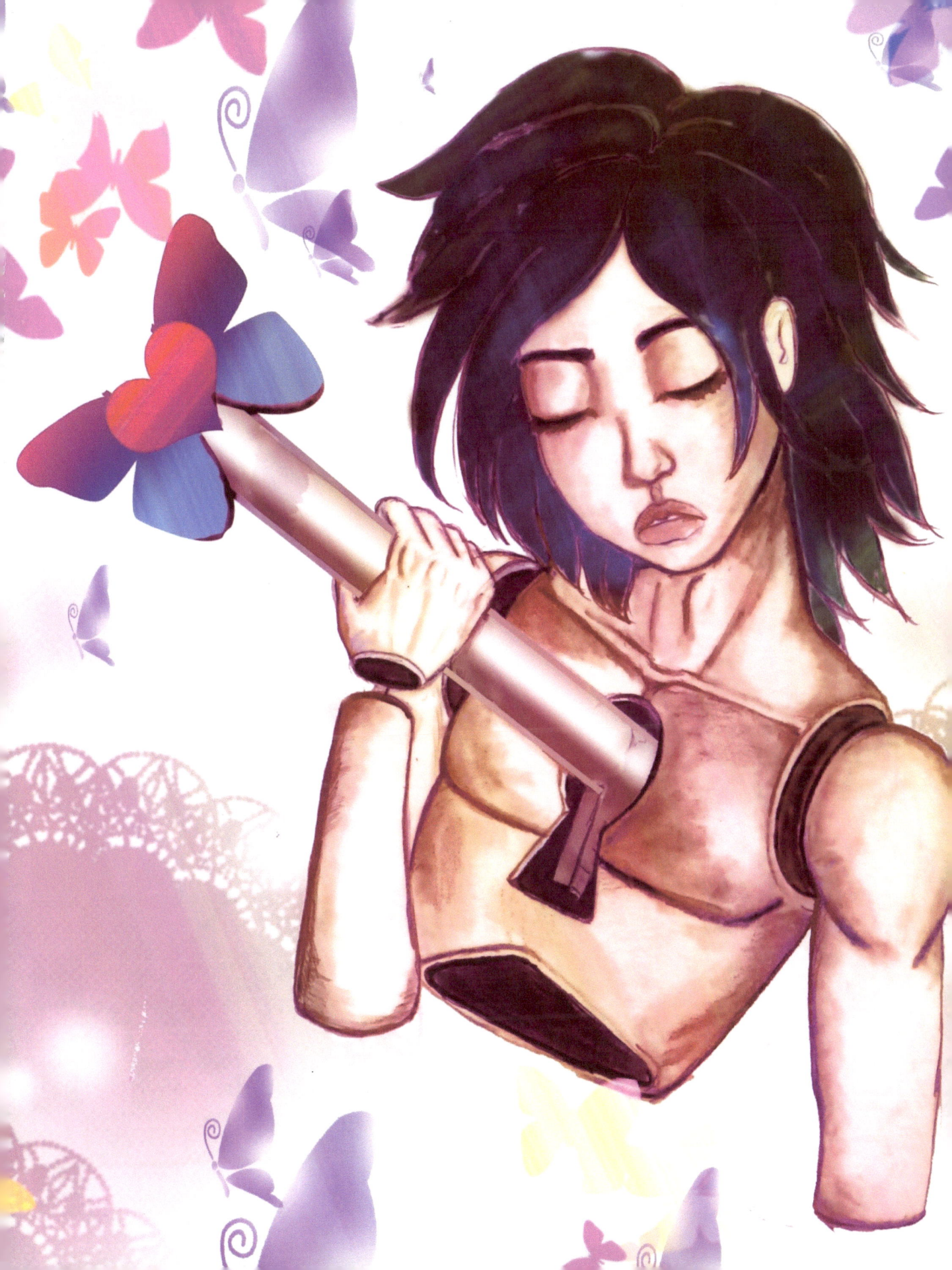

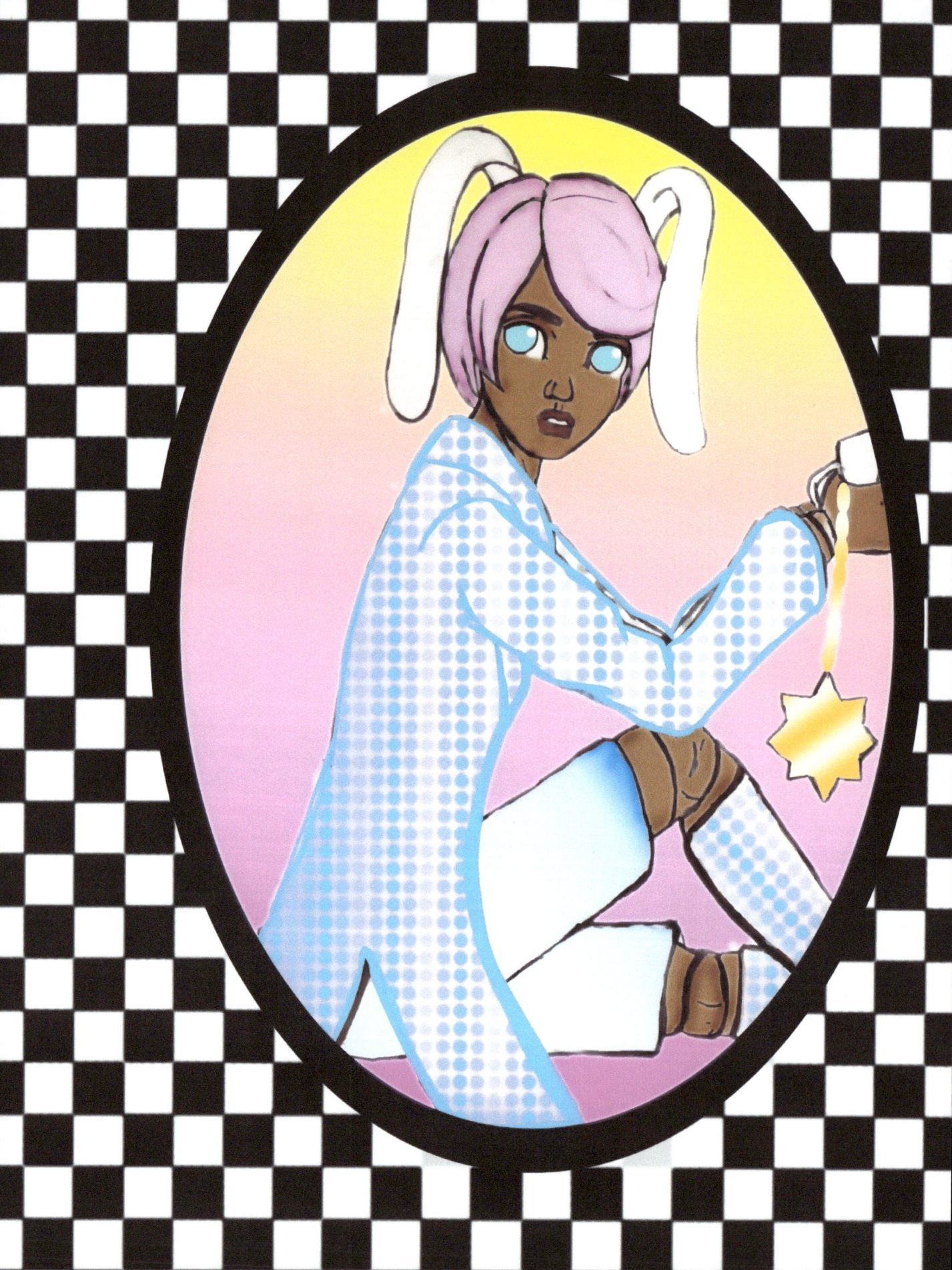

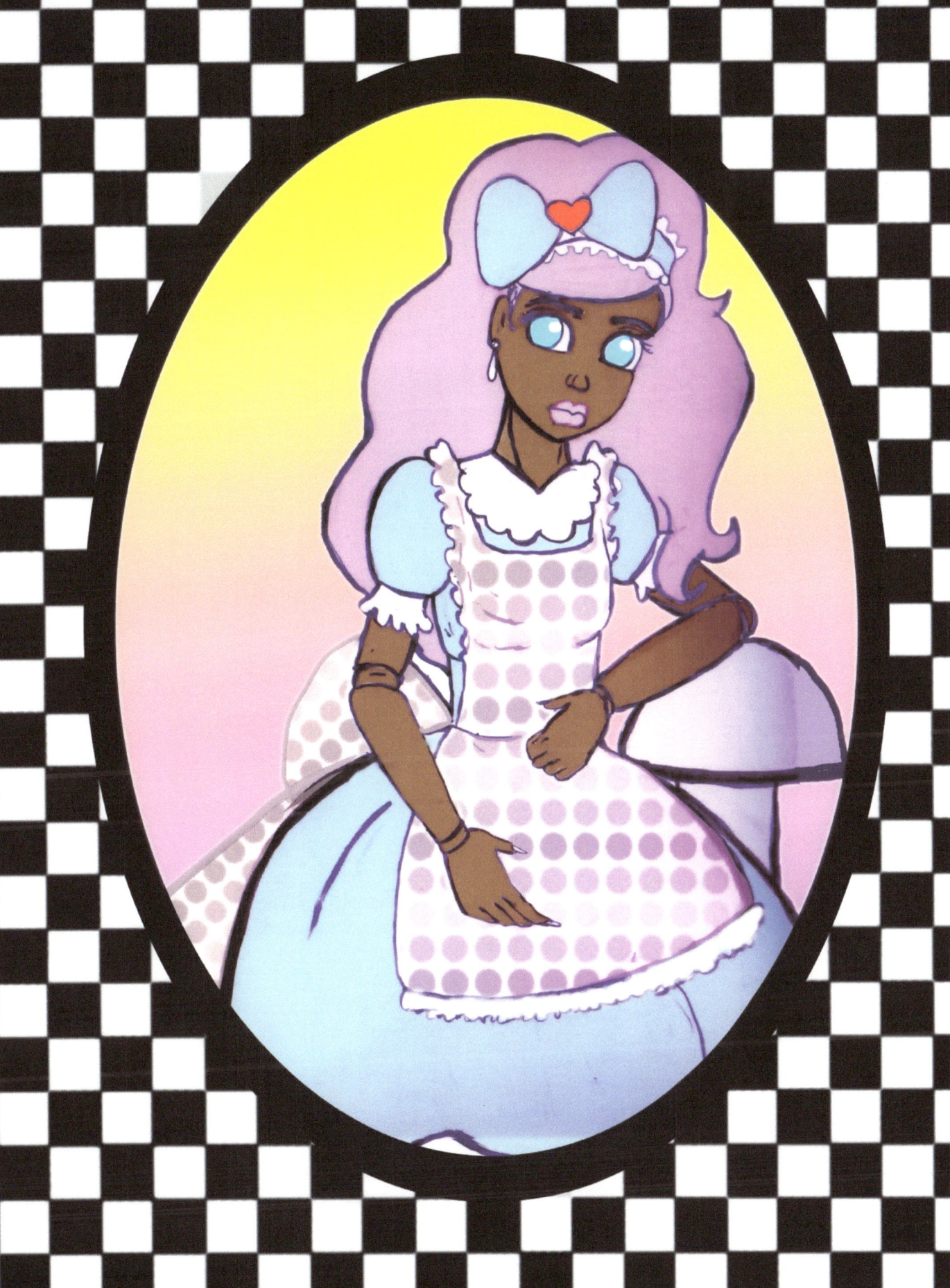

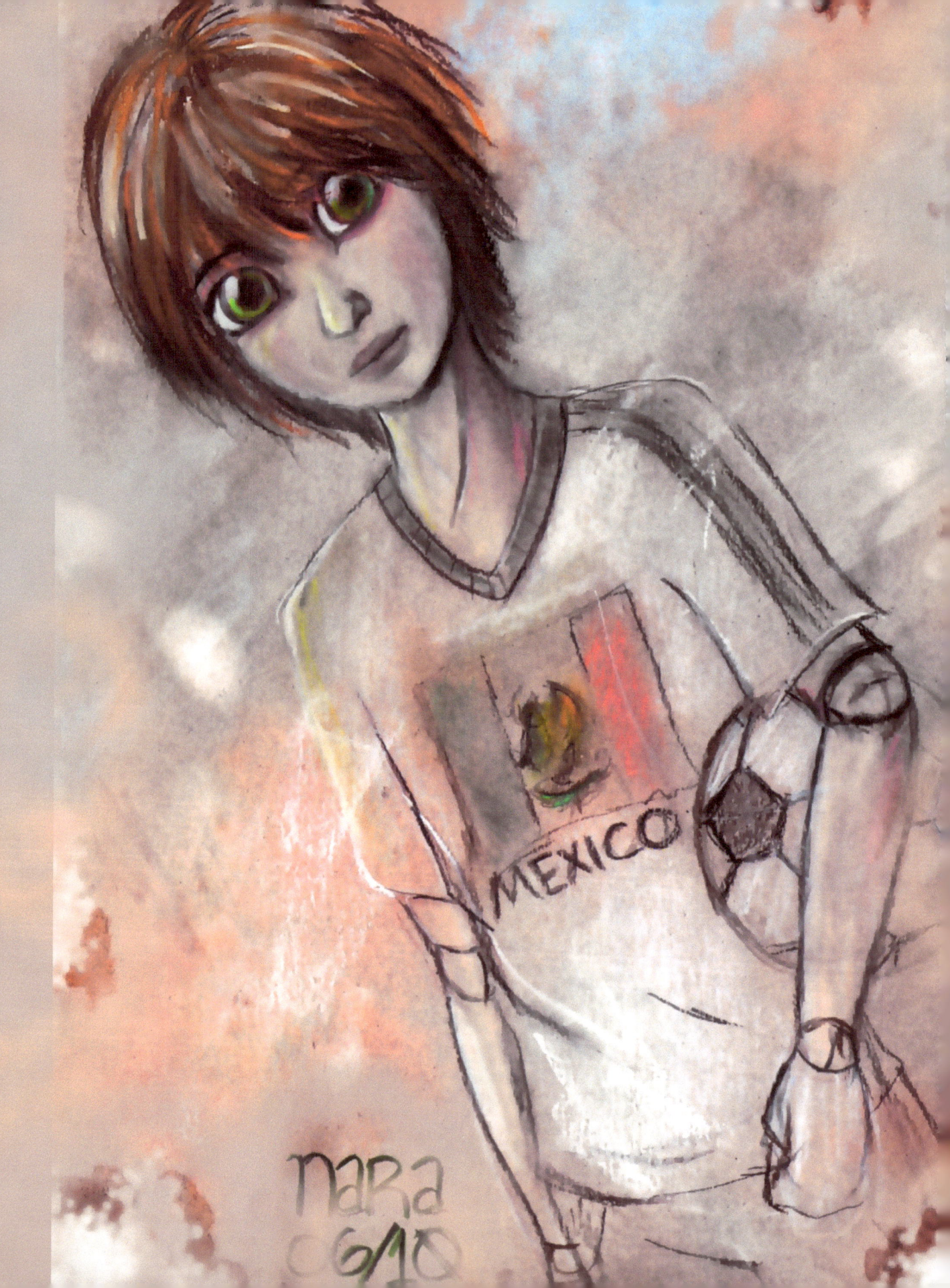

www.ingramcontent.com/pod-product-compliance
Lightning Source LLC
Chambersburg PA
CBHW050909180526
45159CB00007B/2843